THE PRINCESS SAVES HERSELF IN THIS ONE
Copyright © 2016 Amanda Lovelace

Second edition.

ISBN-10: 1532913680
ISBN-13: 978-1532913686

the
princess
saves
herself
in
this
one

for the boy who lived.
thank you for inspiring me to be
the girl who survived.
you may have
a lightning bolt
to show for it
but my body is a
lightning storm.

table of contents

I. the princess . . . . 9 - 37

II. the damsel . . . . 38 - 87

III. the queen . . . . 88 - 128

IV. you . . . . 129 – 153

here lies
the raw,
unpolished,
& mostly
disjointed
pieces of
my soul.

ah, life—
the thing
that happens
to us
while we're off
somewhere else
blowing on
dandelions
& wishing
ourselves into
the pages of
our favorite
fairy tales.

once upon a time...

I. the princess

~~the princess~~ i was born
a little bookmad.

i could be found stroking
the spines of my books

while i sat locked alone
inside my ~~tower~~ bedroom.

all the while, i hoped my books
would spill their exquisite words

over the lush green carpet
so i could collect them one by one

& savor them like
berries inside of my mouth.

- forever a collector of words.

when i had
no friends
i reached inside
my beloved
books
& sculpted some
out of
12 pt
times new roman.

- & it was almost good enough.

~~the queen~~
my mother
smiled
as she offered
a cube of
sugar
in her
upturned palm.

greedily,
i accepted.

i reached inside
my mouth,
delicately placing one
(just one)
on the center
of my tongue,
& i clamped
down.

salt.

that is what abuse is:
knowing you are
going to get salt
but still hoping for sugar
for nineteen years.

- *you may be gone, but i still have a stomachache.*

one night,
~~the princess~~
~~i~~
~~the princess~~
~~i~~
~~the princess~~
~~i~~

the princess woke
to feel the bed rocking

    back & forth
back & forth
       back & forth

            back & forth
         back & forth
              back & forth

    back & forth
back & forth
       back & forth

at first,
she thought
a hurricane
must be brewing—

- i can't. i'm sorry.

you should never love
anything
more than you love
your own children.

you should never love
anyone
more than you love
your own children.

- how could you?

where
do all the
memories go,
the ones we
hide away
with
lock &
key yet
continue
to shape
us all the
s a m e?

- did it really happen if i can't remember it?

at eleven years old
the doctor weighed me
& afterwards,
my mother told me
i was too fat
& that i needed to
go on a diet
immediately.
for an entire year,
food barely passed
through my lips.
i did not even allow myself
to take a sip of water
because i wanted to be
so thin that i
could blow away
with the slightest breeze—
disappear.
i dropped sixty pounds
in a few short months
& i had to wear long sleeves
to cover up the
"cat scratches."

- *everybody told me how good i looked, though.*

"friend request from _____"

a) the girl who said you were ugly.
b) the girl who said your voice was off-key.
c) the girl who refused to defend you.
d) the girl who laughed at you behind your back & to your face.
e) the girl who took your lunch money every day because she said you didn't need to eat.
f) the girl who said you were "fat" even after you starved yourself half to death.
g) the girl who was supposed to be your best friend.
h) all of the above.

- keep pressing ignore, lovely.

fat
/fat/
adjective

    1. a descriptive word.
        it has no deeper meaning.
        it should not determine
        the worth
        (or lack thereof)
        of a human being.

- what i know now that i wish i knew then.

sticks & stones
never broke

                    my bones,

but words
made me
starve myself
until

                  you could
                  see all of them.

- *skin & bone.*

my sister & i
spent our nights
wishing upon
the plastic
glow-in-the-dark
stars
plastered to our
ceiling.

- *we made it after all.*

there
was never
enough alcohol
to keep my mother warm
in a house
as cold as
t h i s.

- *but you kept trying, didn't you?*

there were
once
~~six~~ five
girls
who
shared
every part
of themselves:

          blood
          &
          secrets
          &
          lovers
          &
          even
          a diary.

but
a girl
can only
bleed
so much
before she
meets
her demise.

- *i'll see you in california.*

how can
someone
be
too young
to be
in love
when we were
crafted
from
            ocean waves
            & starlight?

- *young love.*

my first kiss:
>tackled,
>pinned down,
>a mouth
>repeating
>*no no no.*

after:

>bruises
>&
>the unmistakable
>taste of
>blood.

- i will never forgive you.

you have
been the
star
of each
& every
one of
my
nightmares.

- *you left but you stayed.*

i'm sorry
i wasn't
the daughter
you had
in mind.

- *i only ever wanted to make you proud.*

I.
blood
blooming
underneath
the stinging
bite
of steel.

II.
the
once too-tight
jeans
hanging
off
my body.

- *two unexpected reliefs of a girl.*

it is strange
how

s
i
s
t
e
r
s

can
be

s
a
v
i
o
r
s

or

s
t
r
a
n
g
e
r
s

&
sometimes
a bit of both.

- *sisters.*

- silence has always been my loudest scream.

birds
can't
                f l y a w a y
when you
clip
one of
their wings.

you
weren't
satisfied
with just
clipping
one of
my wings.

you tore
both wings
out from
the root
to make sure
i could
                n e v e r f l y
anywhere
ever
again.

- *mother & daughter.*

30

since
i couldn't
have
my wings,
i wore
the
fake ones
dipped
in
gold
glitter.

- *a wannabe faerie in converse.*

there came
a time
when
poetry
showed me
how to
bleed
without
the demand
of blood.

- *my most loyal lover.*

i used to think
i was broken

because
i never once

spent my
daydreams

plucking
swollen pomegranates

from
someone else's tree.

- *then i learned that society is broken, not me.*

watching
the house
that was
my sanctuary
& my hell
go up in
flames
was
bittersweet
but mostly

just
sweet.

- *a confession.*

if a house
does not
automatically
make a home,
then a body
doesn't
automatically
make a home
either.

- *i've always felt like a stranger in my skin.*

you may
not have left
(many) bruises
on my skin,
but you left giant
blackberry bruises
all over
my soul.

- *i still wonder who i would have been.*

the princess
locked herself away
in the highest tower,
hoping a knight
in shining armor
would come to her
rescue.

- i didn't realize i could be my own knight.

II. the damsel

the damsel
let the dragons
swoop down
& steal her away
from the ugliness
of her world.
unbeknownst to her,
she was only trading
one tower
for another.

- *the wickedest liars of all.*

i'm not scared
of the monsters

hidden underneath
my bed.

i'm much more scared
of the boys

with messy brown hair,
sleepy eyes,

& mouths
that only know

how to form
half-truths.

- *my dragons.*

remember when
you told me
you wrote that
beautiful song
for me
& only me—
your
"only one"?

well,

i'm willing
to bet
you don't
remember
that you had already
showed it to me,
saying it was
for *her*.

- *you were in love with the idea of love, not me.*

promises
whispered
in the rain
will be washed

a

w

a

y.

- *right down the fucking drain.*

i was the one thing
he had to deny—
the beautiful truth
within his
terrible lie.

- who knew such a young heart could shatter?

when
my dragon
with the
green eyes
left,

i
took
a knife
& cut off
all my long,
pretty hair,
taking away
the only thing
he
ever
loved
about
me.

- *over before it began.*

"i
could
just
eat
you
up."

- *from the insatiable mouth of the big, bad wolf.*

he loves me.
he loves me not.

        he loves her.
        he loves her not.

he loves me.
he loves me not.

        he loves her.
        he loves her not.

he loves me.
he loves me not.

        he loves her.
        he loves her not.

he loves me.
he loves me not.

        he loves her.
        he loves her not.

he loves me.
he loves me not.

- i ran out of petals.

blood
runs
wherever
his
fingertips
graze
me.

- *my steel & thorns.*

for a time,
it seemed to me
that we were

              starlight-touched,

failing to
realize that
we were actually

              star-crossed.

- the stars were never on our side.

he was made of fire
& i was made of ice.

i came too close to
his flame

& he melted me
with his embers,

reducing me down
to a puddle.

with time,
i froze over again,

but i was never
quite the same—

a fragile, watery imitation
of what once was.

- *where was my fear of fire when it came to you?*

"i hate you."

- *his version of "i love you."*

when
it finally
came
time for
him to
leave,
he
packed up
all my
poetry
in a
suitcase
& took it
with
him.

- *first my heart, then my words.*

he
promised
to fix me
&

                  he left me

more

                  s h a t t e r e d

than i had been
before.

- *but now i've got gold in the cracks.*

i have
so much love
to give,
but no one
ever wants
it.

- *a cup overfilled.*

if
love
is a
battlefield,
then i
must have
forgotten
all of
my armor
at
home.

- *a war i never agreed to fight.*

i spent
my dreams
picking
my teeth
out of
the
carpet.

- *what does dream dictionary say?*

my
mom
told the
nice doctor
she was seeing
starbursts
in her eyes
& they were
almost
beautiful
to her—
like the
fourth of
july
had decided
to come
early.

the doctor
hesitated
before
breaking the news
to her.

"those aren't
stars.

it's cancer."

- *40 years a smoker.*

it was
while we were
drinking our
usual
late night
coffee.
without
a tremble
in that
gravelly voice
of hers,
she turned
to me
& said
her last
dying wish
was for me
to spread her ashes
over the ocean
so she could
finally go
back
home.

- *a mermaid escapist.*

when your mother
begins to forget
your name,
you begin
to wonder
if you exist
at all.

- stage 4, terminal.

irony:
when your
healthy
& intelligent
& strikingly
beautiful
sister dies
less than
a month
before
your terminally ill
mother.

- *nobody realized you were just as sick.*

minutes
before
your mother
made the
death call,

i
smelled
your
warm vanilla
perfume

& my
mouth
filled with
the taste
of dirt.

- *death is one of the senses.*

children are not
meant to die
before their
parents.

i was not
meant to grow
older than
my oldest sister.

we were meant
to be
four sisters,
not three.

you were not meant
to be a can of ashes
on your mother's
bedside table.

after all,
you were the one
who always burned
the brightest.

- *fate is a fucking lie.*

the worst
part is never
being able
to know
if it was a
           s u i c i d e
or not.

- the truth will free me.

she
once
made a
promise
to
save
me

when
all
along

we
should have
been
saving
her
from
herself.

- *please come back.*

sister—
wherever
you are now,
i hope there is
a beach.

- *starfish will always remind me of you.*

fuck you,
cancer,

for taking away
the possibility

of the mother
i will never

ever get to
have now.

- 11/03/10.

your
death certificate
makes
the claim
that
you died on
november 3rd
at 3:03 AM.
that is a
lie.
you died
long
before that.

- *3 isn't my lucky number anymore.*

when
a loved one
dies,
they say
you should
open a window
to let out
that final
wheezing
breath
so their soul
can
be
set free,
but hers is
still here
with me.
night
after night
after night,
she pounds
her fists
on the walls
of my dreams,
begging for
me to tell
her
the way
               out.

- *the other side.*

one funeral:
    tears of grief
    for a life lost
    too young,
    too soon—
    a tragedy.

the other:
    tears of relief
    for a suffering
    that lasted
    far too long—
    a mercy.

- & yet both hollowed me out.

for the
better half
of a year
i was terrified
every time
the phone rang
in case
it was another
death call.

- *3 more would come.*

everyone i love leaves.

how many
funerals can
someone attend
before they turn
nineteen?

- *the cursed family.*

grief
clung to
her
like an
old,
itchy,
faded,
ill-fitting,
hand-me-down
dress.

death

wound

itself

around

her

bones

like

a

piece

of

red

ribbon.

i never
expected
death
to be my most
faithful companion,
but she is
the only one
who will come
without
having to be
asked.

- *the only one who will never leave.*

is
there
such a
thing
as
dead
mother's day?

months after
my mom
died,
i found the book
she was
reading
last
with a yellowing
receipt
still tucked inside,
marking her place,
& it finally
hit me

you
will never
get to finish
this particular book
you will never
get to start
or finish
another book
ever again
you will never
get to see me
graduate
from college
you will never
meet the love
of my life
you will never
be there for my
wedding
you will never
read these words

we will never
ever ever ever
sit on the back porch
& swap ghost stories
over steaming
coffee mugs
ever
ever
ever
again.

she
won't
stop
haunting
me.

- *my ghost.*

he
won't
stop
hunting
me.

- my ghost II.

fuck the idea
that there is
such a thing
as destiny,
that there exists
some kind of
mysterious master plan,
that there is a god who
simply
does not
give us anything
we cannot
handle.

the pain
did not
make me
a better person.
it did not
teach me not to
take anything
for granted.
it did not
teach me anything
except how
to be afraid
to love anyone.

i am
far too
young
to be so
goddamn
broken
&

if i could go back
in time
& give
myself
her childhood
back,

      i would.

- *what was the point?*

maybe
i find it
so hard to
believe in

                heaven

because
i don't know
if there

                will be
                poetry

there.

- legitimate concerns of a mortal.

i had a
big smile
on my face
as i burned
the bridges
to all the things
i could not
repair.

- *does the smoke still choke you?*

it took
        losing him
        to finally
        find
        myself.

it took
        losing him
        a second time
        to be sure
        of myself.

that
        was my
        first act
        of
        self-love.

- *i would thank you, but we both know you don't
deserve it.*

who would
i have
been without
the inspiration
behind my

        demons?

- *probably not a poet.*

i am
caught between
mourning
you

&

thinking
your death
saved
me.

- *will you ever be able to forgive me?*

the princess
jumped from
the tower
& she
learned
that she
could fly
all along.

- *she never needed those wings.*

III. the queen

once upon
a time,
the princess
rose from the ashes
her dragon lovers
made of her
&
crowned
herself
the
mother-fucking
queen of
herself.

- *how's that for a happily ever after?*

in my
mind's eye
i always see you
sitting by yourself
at the kitchen table,
smoking your cigarette
& drinking your coffee
& wanting to be
anywhere else
but here
with
us.

- *were you set free?*

maybe
we will meet again
in another place—
a place where
forgiveness grows
as lovely as
the tomatoes
used to grow
in your
garden.

- *the shiny red hope that gets me through late
nights.*

when
my mother
died
i finally
got to
meet
my father,
who i
had seen
every day
for
nineteen
years.

it's true
what they
say:
the weight
of
shared
grief
can either
bring you
together
or
drive
you apart.

- *it's never too late for a relationship.*

when you choose
to sit upon a
throne
made up of
lies

&
the bodies
of the people who
mistakenly thought
they could

t
r
u
s
t

you,
the only
thing left
to do
is

f
a
l
l.

- *but i bet it was fun while it lasted.*

what ever
will you do
when everyone
stops believing
your
red lipstick
stained
lies?

- *friends can break your heart, too.*

i bet
you regret
making
an enemy
out of
me.

- *1 back, 2 knives.*

i wonder
how many times
you touched her
& had to
pretend
it was
me.

- *does it still sting?*

i hope you
treat her better
than you
ever
treated me.

- *you can have my forgiveness, but you can't
have me.*

please
believe me
when i say
revenge
was
never
my intention.

- *but it still tastes sweeter than honey.*

you   the
brought   needle
& i brought the thread.
we meant to mend our
two broken hearts,
but we ended up
stitching them
togeth
er.

if he was
my cup of tea,
then you are
my cup of
coffee.

tea simply
isn't
enough
for me
sometimes,

but
coffee
can get me
through
anything.

- *did i make you up?*

before he left,
he wrapped my heart
in layers of
briars & barbed wire
to make sure
that no one else
could ever get in,
but you were
more than willing
to bloody
your hands
for me.

- *you never even got pricked.*

his talent:

he never
once
had to use
his hands
to touch
each & every
part of
me.

- *he could touch me across highways.*

somehow,
my soul
knew
your soul
before we
ever
met.

- *it was like coming home after a long, long day.*

I.   he calls me
        gorgeous.

II.   he reads
        all my
        favorite books
        & then
        asks for
        more.

III.   he knows
        exactly how
        to make my coffee.
        ("light & sweet,
        just like you," i
        always joke to him.)

IV.   he asks me
        how i am doing
        every single day
        & he
        genuinely
        cares to hear
        the answer.

V.   best of all,
        i know he will
        still love me
        when he
        wakes up
        tomorrow morning.

- 5 things you made me think weren't possible.

i say to him,

"we will always
have our octobers.

- *even when everything else fades.*"

he
opened me up
like a book
& poured the
poetry
back into
me.

- *my personal pen & paper.*

a list of red things:
        I. his hair.
        II. our lips.
        III. my nails.
        IV. our breath.
        V. my sheets.

- *worth the wait.*

flowers
grow
wherever
his
fingertips
graze
me.

- *my sun & rain.*

t
h
i
s
:
you & me,
a fading october afternoon,
the biting chill filling up the air,
noses turning rosy at the tips,
drinking our too-sweet coffees,
pinkies hooked together,
forgetting everything
& everyone else.
this, this,
this.

- 10/13/12

he is
even better
than books.

- *fiction has nothing on you.*

i am so glad
we were born
during the same
lifetime.

- i may not believe in fate, but i believe in you.

his smile makes my bones ache.

- *a pain i welcome.*

when i see
your light pieces
with
my dark pieces,
i begin to
understand why
they say
opposites attract.

- *chiaroscuro.*

i am so sorry
for all the times
the

           darkling
           dragon
           demon

living inside
my darkest
corners
came
roaring out,
flames ready,
hell-bent
on
extinguishing

           all the light
           in you.

- *please don't leave.*

the constellation
of stars
       s c a t t e r e d
across his
back
is the
map
that guides me
home
each time
i find myself
lost.

- *you are my home.*

he
did not
teach me
how
to love
myself,
but he
was
the bridge
that
helped me
get

       here.

- i thank the universe every day for you.

he walked
me down
the bridge
marked with
our names,
got down
on one
knee,
& opened up
my favorite
book—
the one
with the
beautiful princess
& her own
beloved book
on the cover.

inside,
i found

a tiny,
perfect,
amethyst
hope.

- 't will forever keep.

i
let myself
know
that my life
doesn't
have to be over
just because
theirs are
& i went
ahead
& painted
the sun
back into
my sky.

- *i am allowed to live my life.*

"what are you
going to do with your
english degree?"

"i plan to
crack open
the skulls of the
masses
& plant
a colorful
garden
in every
brain."

"i am
going to lace
together
a necklace
of words
for everyone
i meet."

"for once
in my life
i am going
to make sure
someone finally
hears
me."

"i don't know."

- & it's okay not to know.

fiction:
        the ocean
        i dive
        headfirst
        into
        when i
        can
        no longer
        breathe
        in
        reality.

- *a mermaid escapist II.*

i would like to eat
one meal
without feeling
                    ashamed.

- *healing is ongoing.*

all of the oceans
& galaxies
did not
conspire together to
create me
just so i could
reproduce for
you.

- *startling fact #1.*

if i ever
have a
daughter,
the first
thing
i will
teach her
to love
will be
the word
"no"
&
i will
not
let her feel
guilty
for using
it.

- *"no" is short for "fuck off."*

i am
a tigress
who has earned
her softer-than-velvet
stripes.

- an ode to my stretchmarks.

i am
a lioness
who is no longer
afraid to let the world
hear her
roar.

- an ode to me.

when i die,
do not
waste
a minute
mourning me.
i may go,
but i will
leave behind
all my
thousand & one
lives.

- *a bookmad girl never dies.*

i
hope
you
can find it
in your
heart
to be
proud
of the
woman
i have become
in spite
of
you.

- *still hoping for sugar instead of salt.*

i will
take the
blood-tipped
thorns
they
stuck
in you
&
from
them
i will
teach you
how to
weave
together
the crown
you
deserve.

- *you are stronger than i will ever know.*

IV. you

raid your library.
read everything
you can get your
hands on
& then
some.

go on,
collect words
& polish them up
until they shine
like starlight
in your
palm.

make words
your finest weapons—
a gold-hilted sword
to cut your
enemies
         d
           o
             w
                n.

- a survival plan of sorts.

trees
have words
the wind
cannot carry,
so we must
write
on them
their stories
until there are
none left
for them
to tell.

- *write the story.*

write the story.

push
your hands
into the dirtiest
parts of yourself.

take the
rot & decay
& turn it into
nourishment & life.

water it
& sing to it
& show it
sunlight.

grow a beautiful garden
from your aching
& teach yourself
how to thrive from it.

write your story.

- the sign you've been waiting for.

1. fill in the blank:
   a) poetry is _____.

      - anything you want it to be.

when you live
in new york
or new jersey

it is almost
a rite of passage
when someone
jumps in front
of your train.

the first thought
is always,
"i'm going to be
late for work."
it is never,
"what a tragedy
she felt that
there was no
other way out."

but it is.
it is a fucking
tragedy
when
the world
does not stop
for you
even when
you give it
every last
drop of your
blood.

- *i never learned your name, but you mattered to me.*

there is not
enough
rain water
in all
the skies
to rinse
the
innocent
blood
from
your hands.

- *their lives will always matter.*

a
world
where all

human beings
are taken care of

shouldn't be called

a "revolutionary"
way of life

& yet
it is.

- *burn.*

if you
don't want to
end up in
someone else's
poem,
then maybe
you should

            start
            treating
            people
            better
            for
            a
            change.

- an unapologetic poet.

emily—
i often
find myself
wondering
if you are still
out there
with lanterns,
looking for
yourself.

is sylvia there
with you,
guiding
the way by
the old
brag
of her
beating
heart?

does
virginia
have
a room
all her own?
& what about
harriet
& anne
& harper?

does
a woman
ever
find
her peace?

is death
our only
feather-covered
hope?

- *i'll be there with matches.*

your hips
will try to burst
through your skin.

your thighs
will try to grow together
like a mermaid's tail.

a soft garden
will try to sprout
on your legs.

(& between your legs,
on your upper lip,
on your armpits, etc.)

no, you are
not just here to be
sexy for him.

the world begins
& ends
when you say so.

- *what they don't want you to know.*

food
is
not
the
enemy.

- *society is.*

i'm
pretty sure
you have

        s t a r d u s t

running
through
those

        v e i n s.

- *women are some kind of magic.*

you
are not
obligated
to have
children
just because
your body
has that
capability.

you
are so
so
so
much more
than the
possibility
of
children.

you give
birth
to oceans

every
single
day.

- your friendly neighborhood man-hater & child-eater.

be a
mermaid.

be a mermaid
who doesn't settle
for making a
small splash.

be a
mermaid
who doesn't
stop until she makes
tidal waves.

be a
mermaid
who knows to
stop before
she devastates
the world with her
tsunamis.

- don't allow the world to take your kindness.

you
did
absolutely
nothing
to
deserve
it.

- fuck rape culture.

repeat after me:
you owe
no one
your
forgiveness.

- *except maybe yourself.*

the love
some girls
have for
other girls
is
so gentle
& so soft
& so fucking
beautiful,
&
these girls
deserve
to have
better stories
than the ones
where they
are murdered
because they love
with too much
of their
hearts.

- *love is never a weakness.*

the only thing
required
to be
a woman
is to
identify
as one.

- *period, end of story.*

your happiness
comes before
anyone else's
happiness.

- the real meaning of "self-respect."

just because
they don't
hit you
doesn't mean it
isn't
abuse.

wouldn't you
think it
a crime
to look up
at
the night sky
& tell
the stars
that they have
no sparkle?

guess what?
you shine
brighter
than all the
starlight
there has
ever been
or ever
will be.

- *emotional abuse is still abuse.*

you deserve
someone
who makes
you feel
like the
otherworldly
creature
you are.

- *yourself.*

be wary
of the boys who
only ever tell
half-truths
because they
will only ever be
half in love
with you.

- slay those dragons.

when
someone
offers to
save you
make it
your mission
to
save yourself.

- i believe in you.

the end.

special acknowledgements

I.   *my sun & rain,* who believed i could write this even when i didn't.

II.   *my father,* who probably didn't know i was a writer but will hopefully be proud of me for writing this.

III.   *my sister-savior,* who wouldn't imagine giving up on me even in the darkest of times.

IV.   *the rest of my family,* who always encouraged me to keep moving forward even if it meant pushing me out of my comfort zone.

V.   *my beta readers (christine, mira, danika, shauna, rob, mason, & lauren),* who cried while reading this & – most importantly – pointed out my inconsistences & corrected most of my grammar mistakes.

about the author

amanda lovelace is a poetess & storyteller whose words have been shared in her local coffee shop & her tumblr blogs. she currently lives in new jersey with her fiancé. she received her A.A. in english literature from brookdale community college in 2014. as of 2016, she is working toward her B.A. in english literature & sociology at kean university. what she will do next, nobody knows—not even her. for now, you can find her reading anything she can get her hands on, writing while she should probably be paying attention in class, thinking about writing but not actually writing, drinking an inordinate amount of coffee, & blogging about books. on top of all this she is a lover of all things cat-related as well as a staunch mermaid enthusiast. she considers herself to be a feminist & a social justice advocate. you can also find her as *ladybookmad* on twitter, instagram, & tumblr.

38724434R00088

Made in the USA
Middletown, DE
24 December 2016